presents…

The Perfect Soccer Player Blueprint:

Master the <u>9 Keys</u> to soccer success -

Become the best player on the field every game.

Ross LaBauex

Quincy Amarikwa

TABLE OF CONTENTS

BONUS/WHO ARE WE?

Thank you for purchasing our book! Quincy and I (Ross) have compiled PDF print outs, videos of drills, detailed examples and more you can use to greatly improve the 9 key aspects of your game we discuss in this book.

To get access to these FREE resources please head over to:

http://www.PerfectSoccerPlayer.com/Bonus

Who are we, and why should you even listen to us?

Ross LaBauex and Quincy Amarikwa are current professional soccer players in Major League Soccer. Combined, we have won at the highest levels achievable in US soccer both collegiately and professionally –winning a Division 1 NCAA Men's National Championship and a MLS Cup Championship along the way.

Ross LaBauex

Quincy Amarikwa

On top of being college soccer and Major League Soccer champions, here a few things we've collectively achieved in the game:

4-year College Letterman,
2-year College Captain,
1 time All-ACC,
2009 ACC Tournament Champion,
NSCAA All American,
College GOTY 2008,
2009 Big West Offensive Player Of The Year,
2009 Big West Leading Goal and Points Leader,
2009 NCAA Top 10 Goals In The Country,
MLS Club Goal Leader 2014,
MLS Club Leader in Points 2014,
MLS Most Fouled Player 2014,
Volkswagen Man Of The Match 2014,
MLS All Star Nominee,
5 Time MLS Goal Of The Week Nominee,
MLS Team Of The Week…

We share these other accomplishments not to brag, but to show you that when it comes to soccer you can trust that we know what we're talking about. There are many "pro" or "ex-pro" players claiming to know and teach what it takes to play at a high level, but when you take a deeper look at their credentials they; only went on trial with a pro team, played semi-pro, or would have gone pro but xyz happened so it didn't work out.

This is the very reason we decided it was time to step in and teach what it really takes to play, since we've actually done it for ourselves.

We have a deep passion for the game of soccer because it has allowed us so many great opportunities and experiences that at one time we thought to be unimaginable. Our mission is to offer solutions for players, parents, and youth coaches that want to help their soccer dreams become a reality.

Our goal is to help as many players as possible play at the highest level possible!

http://www.PerfectSoccerPlayer.com/Bonus

.

FOR GRABBING A COPY OF OUR BOOK WE'D ALSO LIKE TO EXTEND YOU A 10% DISCOUNT **CODE: PS9KEYS** TO ANY AND ALL SOCCER TRAINING EQUIPMENT PURCHASED OVER AT:

http://www.PerfectSoccerSkills.com

INTRODUCTION

Many people are under the impression that becoming a great soccer player is about natural talent. While talent can be a contributing factor, more times than not it is a combination of many different things that determines a players ability to excel on the soccer field. Although talent is required for soccer success, it is <u>always</u> accompanied by multiple other factors. Talent alone is never enough.

All great soccer players have **nine** soccer fundamentals in common. You will find that "talent" is something that comes as a result of the proper implementation of these nine core fundamentals, not the other way around.

Most players make the mistake of thinking that becoming a better player isn't possible for a number of reasons — They think they're not good enough, fast enough, smart enough, or talented enough. The list is endless. When you fully understand and implement the nine fundamentals of soccer success, you will find these reasons to be nothing more than excuses. Great soccer players don't make excuses; they take responsibility for their soccer development and find the solutions to their soccer problems.

This book will give you an overhead view of the nine fundamental keys to soccer success and how to get started improving each one on your journey to becoming a top-level soccer player. Understanding and improving these aspects of your game will set you apart from the majority of your soccer competition, as most players don't fully understand what it is that sets great soccer players apart from the rest.

Having and indeed taking the initiative to develop and progress is fundamental to improving. This book will provide you with the tools required to develop as a soccer player — **the implementation is your responsibility**.

Think of your soccer development like a game of Chess. If you know every possible outcome before you make a decision, you will always have the upper hand. In a similar way, predicting or establishing what is required to improve as a player before your competition, also places you ahead. It's the great soccer players that recognize this and use this knowledge to their advantage — so lets get started.

MENTALITY

The constant unpredictability of soccer is what makes it a very complex, focus driven sport. Your mentality is one of many facets that will help you become a great player, or will be another thing that holds you back.

What's most interesting about soccer is that the mental part is **just as important** as the physical and technical. Unfortunately, many players don't realize this fact. You may feel as though you can't improve the physical and technical –a clear indication in itself of a poor mentality.

Having a good mentality is the catalyst for improving the physical and technical aspects of your game. High performing athletes will initially talk about the work they did in the gym, weight room etc. But, they equally work(ed) on the mental side of the game is well.

Progressing through the ranks to reach a professional level requires determination and dedication. Only those who develop and hone their mental state flourish.

Having a great mentality requires certain characteristics, synonymous with all great athletes. Those characteristics are: **Drive, Focus, Work Rate, Emotional Control, Visualization,** and **Active Preparation.**

Having these be a constant in your psyche can be the difference between winning and losing, being a good player, or being a great player.

The mastery of these characteristics will not happen over night, and require a lot of practice. The first step into achieving mental toughness is the last characteristic listed above – active preparation.

Active preparation is what most times goes unseen. It is what you're willing to do, to become great. A lot of times in soccer, we only ever see the overt forms of preparation through team practice. This is the largest reason players don't improve as soccer players like they should.

Don't get us wrong, team practice is needed and is a great way to supplement your soccer training – but in order to improve your soccer abilities and get to the next level, your preparation needs to go beyond scheduled team practice.

I learned this most from one of my favorite ex-teammates, Pablo Masteroeni. He epitomized what it took to not only become, but remain a great soccer player. He did so by spending extra time perfecting his craft on his own time. Even after being a 2002 World Cup starter and having been capped over 50 times for The United States, Pablo was still willing to do extra work to improve.

From the outside you would think someone like Pablo relied solely on his natural abilities. If I hadn't been on the inside and training with him on a daily basis, I would have never known that it takes countless hours of extra work to get to his level as a player.

In my rookie season, Pablo and I played the same position. Before every practice he would make sure to get touches on the ball through juggling, passing, and different foot skills.

But most importantly AFTER a hard day of practice, Pablo would pull me and a few other players aside to do **even more** technical work. This work varied but usually consisted of different passing patterns, shooting, and movement with and without the ball.

It was as if we hadn't already practiced, Pablo was flying through drills and pushing himself to the limits. That's when I truly realized that players who are the best are the ones doing the most when no one else is watching. His drive, focus, and skill are something I always admired and made me want to push myself to do everything in my power to perfect my craft.

It's what you're willing to do **in addition to** what is required that will determine how good you ultimately become as a soccer player. (And anything else in life for that matter.)

Implementing this characteristic into your mind is pretty straightforward. Remember, little things done consistently over a long duration of time is what yields results.

A few things you can do to help in "active preparation."

1. Write down **what** you want to accomplish during a team practice, individual practice, game.

For Example: "In team practice I want to improve my communication with my center back partner."

2. Write **how** you will accomplish these goals.

For Example: "I will accomplish this goal by making sure that whenever an opposing player is in the area, I will be vocal so that everyone on the field can hear me."

3. Evaluate your goals.

For Example: "Today I did an average job of communicating with my center back partner. I was not vocal enough when players were making runs and as a result, we conceded two goals. What I need to implement in the future is have my teammates constantly remind me that I need to be vocal so it becomes natural. I also can let my coach know I am working on being a vocal leader on the field and if he/she sees times where I am not being vocal, I will ask them to address it.

Drive is very important in soccer. What is your driving force? What makes you motivated to be great? What makes you excited to get up every morning and accomplish your goals?

For many, the love of the game is enough, but for others, they have ulterior driving forces. Whatever you decide on, make sure you remind yourself **why** you are doing everything you do. A great way to reinforce this is by physically speaking it, or even writing it down somewhere that you can often see it –particularly when things seem hard.

We have found that doing this makes it easier to have direction, to stay organized, and to stay positive. Whenever you're struggling for meaning or you're lost, refer back to the reason you play soccer.

I remember my first season of College Soccer being very difficult. I was young and not playing in as many games as I hoped for. At the time I thought I was ready to be in the starting line up and capable of contributing as a Freshman. I ended up only playing 72 minutes for the entire season.

It was a low point for me, because of the fact I wasn't playing, I began to doubt myself. Many different things started to run through my mind: "Did I make the wrong decision on schools?" "Will this get any better?" "Will I ever play at substantial minutes for my college team?"

After a much needed winter break, I refocused and wrote down my "why" for playing college soccer, as well as my short and long-term goals. Doing so helped me really get serious about becoming the type of player a coach wouldn't hesitate to have in his starting lineup.

Focusing on my why is what helped me to formulate and execute a plan that eventually got me into the starting lineup for my remaining 3 years in school.

Everybody experiences doubts and distractions. It is drive that will keep you going when you feel tired, when you want to quit, or when you feel like you have no more to give. Remember, your brain is one of your most important muscles, consistently feed it positive energy…

While working on writing this book, I read a book titled: Everybody Writes by Ann Handley. In it she wrote of an interview she had with a man by the name of Jeff Goins who said,

> "Spending five hours on a Saturday writing isn't nearly as valuable as spending 30 minutes a day every day of the week. Especially when you're just getting started…
> **Practiced once a week aren't habits at all, they're obligations**."

Jeff was obviously speaking with reference to writing, but

what he said really stood out to me because the very same holds true for becoming better as a soccer player. You do not stumble upon success, you earn it over time and your drive is what is going to get you there.

The key is finding out or realizing what your drive or motivating factor is. The very fact that you are reading this now is evidence enough that you have the drive to become the best soccer player you can be, you just need to realize it.

Before starting training, going to the gym, or even playing your next game, stop and think about your driving factor. What is it that makes you want to succeed in soccer so much?

There is no right or wrong answer and each person or teammate may have a completely different reason, but the key is that everybody must have one. Find yours.

Take time to think about the exact reason you started playing to begin with, what the end goal is and why. Once you have, always refer to it. When times get hard, and they will, recall the reason for why you want to do this rather than excuses as to why you don't have to.

Another important note is that this drive can change. Maybe your drive and motivation is to become professional. Once you accomplish this there should be a new drive –be the best on the new team, best in the league, top scorer, whatever works best for you.

Focus. It looks different for everyone, but still has an overlying presence we all can see, and even at times feel. When you look into the eyes of Cristiano Ronaldo, you can see he means business. Yes, he is having fun and enjoying himself, but he is still clearly focused on the task at hand – to play well, and ultimately contribute to the team winning.

The same must go for all players that want to be great. You must be able to focus through all obstacles thrown in front of you, not allowing them to distract you –whether or not they are under your control.

On the field that could be the opposing team doing things to try to throw you off your game –like playing dirty, trash talking, or trying to get the ref on their side.

Off the field that could be: friends, family, school, the press, being lazy, self doubt…

You must not allow any of these things to get the best of you, and understanding every situation that could potentially have you lose your focus is key. You must be able to acknowledge what is occurring and use that to keep your focus.

Simply attempting to block all external stimuli is not sufficient; acknowledgment and **acceptance** is crucial to high performance.

Their isn't one particular way to get better at focusing, but you can make a point to start setting intentions for everything you do. Doing this will allow you to find clarity when obstacles presents themselves and keep you on track to achieving your goals.

It's best to do this for things that are under your control and routed in behavior. For example, before your season starts you can write down goals that you want to set for yourself:

1. I promise to never give up on a play.

2. I will accept criticism and see it as an opportunity to grow as a player.

3. I promise to never miss a training session.

4. I will do 4 hours of extra work outside of practice every week.

5. I will watch 2 professional soccer games a week.

Etc…

Or you could take this further by getting specific to your particular position. If you're a forward, you can tell yourself to make sure you focus on your near post runs every time the ball goes wide. If you're a defender, you can tell yourself to focus on closing the space when the ball is out wide and not letting the winger get crosses into the penalty box. If you're a goal keeper you can tell yourself that you will always be a vocal presence and leader from the back.

The possibilities are endless; just make sure that your intentions are firmly set before you step on the field. This will lead you to place your focus on the particular parts of your game you most want to improve on. Once done long enough these habits turn in to permanent parts of your game –becoming second nature.

Emotional Control is synonymous with being a calm soccer player. Being able to control those emotions over the course of 90 minutes of sprinting, kicking, tackling and words being exchanged, is difficult. When emotions flare, you can see players begin to do things uncharacteristic of themselves.

We saw David Beckham lose his head in the Round of 16 match of the 1998 World Cup against Argentina. Beckham was fouled pretty hard and in a split second he retaliated, resulting in him being sent off the field with a red card. England went on to lose the game in penalties.

Similarly, Zinedine Zidane in the 2006 World Cup Final, exchanged words with an opponent and through frustration, Zidane head butted the player, resulting in a red card.

Zidane's team also went on to lose the match in penalties, it was his last game for his country and a terrible way to bow out, risking tarnishing his world class reputation built over the previous decade.

Some of the best players in the world have lost control of their emotions, so it's definitely possible. But we want to help you not have an outburst that can directly hurt your team. (Which in turn, hurts you.)

<u>Always put the team before yourself, and your ego.</u>

Yes it is ok to be emotional and to wear your heart on your sleeves, at times. But, you must be mindful that there is a time and place for everything. When playing soccer, you need to be even keel. Never riding too high or too low, but somewhere in the middle.

Have you ever heard the saying, "Calm before the storm?" Well soccer is the storm, and being able to be calm throughout is extremely important.

One player that exudes great calmness and even keel is Andres Iniesta. When he plays, you can see that he is always in full control of every situation. With and without the ball he knows exactly what his task is and how to best execute it. He never lets emotions take over on the field, nor does he attempt things that aren't characteristic of his game.

Not falling victim to mental games will show maturity. Coaches want players that are mature –players that can handle all situations the game throws at them. (So do your teammates.) Even the most talented player on the team will not be popular in the locker room if they can not be trusted to not land the team in trouble.

Earning a reputation as a hot head will hurt your career if coaches categorize you as such. Only making your soccer career more difficult before it's even begun.

Like we mentioned earlier, it can be difficult to stay calm at times, but it certainly is not impossible. Work on it, whether that's by not saying something back to a teammate when you mess up, a coach being critical of your play, or even an opponent that will do anything to get under your skin.

Having that emotional control will help you through the ups and downs of the game; control your emotions and watch your game go to the next level.

Visualization, the current Manchester United great Wayne Rooney has gone on record saying,

> "I always like to picture the game the night before. I'll ask the kitman what kit we're wearing, so I can visualize it. It's something I've always done, from when I was a young boy. It helps to train your mind to situations that might happen the following day. I think about it as I'm lying in bed. What will I do if the ball gets crossed in the box this way? What movement will I have to make to get on the end of it? Just different things that might make you one per cent sharper."

Visualizing in soccer is something a majority of great players do. Like Wayne Rooney said, it helped train his mind to situations that might happen during the game.

David Beckham is another who openly stated that this was a big part of his game. Specifically, he would visualize taking free kicks the night before, seeing the ball curl over the wall and into the goal. Picturing his foot striking the ball at the perfect angle as it rises and then dips under the crossbar.

Even before taking free kicks in the game, he would revert to this method, taking a few seconds to recall the images before physically taking the kick.

This is a great way to increase the positive thoughts that are going to help you be mentally strong and have confidence to perform tasks during a game. Constant visualization will result in you feeling like you have been in game situations thousands of times, helping you feel confortable and react to situations as second nature once actually in them.

Still, more goes into the game than just visualization, and only imagining scoring a goal is not sufficient enough to make it happen. You still have to put the work in, on and off the field if you want to see things come to fruition.

If you're a defender, maybe you visualize yourself making a great tackle, or whipping in a great cross and the team scoring. If you're a goalkeeper, maybe its making a game winning save. Or maybe just making all the saves you should make.

Whatever it may be, we encourage you to envision what you would like to do on the field, and then work to implement it on the practice field, and ultimately in to the game.

Work Rate is essential not only in dedicating time to improve these mental aspects but the physical as well.

Some of the most talented players in professional soccer never had a fraction of the career success they could have had, with the addition of a simple work rate.

A perfect example of this is Matt Le Tissier, an English soccer player from the start of the Premier League era. Largely considered the most naturally talented soccer player of his generation, the midfielder managed just 8 games for England in his 16-year professional career.

The reason attributed to this was that he was deemed lazy and a luxury player that needed his teammates to do the work for him and simply give him the ball. While his club coach was prepared to structure the whole team around this, the England national team was not and he was constantly excluded from the side.

He also stayed at an average league club his whole career, not making the move to any bigger sides.

There is absolutely **zero** excuse for not developing your work rate as a player. In no situation will a high work rate be classified as a negative by a coach or by any of your teammates. Even better, work rate is a <u>mentality</u>.

Every single person, regardless of talent, has the same ability to dedicate him or herself and improve their work rate. Put the work in on the training field, and in the gym and your game will improve. It is one of the most simple equations possible, put enough physical work in and the result is guaranteed.

Additionally, soccer players that have a visibly high work rate on the pitch are always viewed positively, often actually given more slack for mistakes or poor performances as their work rate exudes the demeanor that they care a great deal about the team and result. This resonates with people and will always benefit the individual player.

Work rate is a huge reason why Quincy remained earning opportunities early on in his professional career –ultimately giving him the opportunity to win a starting spot. This is one thing that is greatly within your control, so take advantage of it!

Bringing it all together:

Everything we've spoken about that makes up a great soccer mentality are all aspects of your game that can be improved upon –that's the good news.

For example to improve heading skills; you can physically perform hundreds of heading drills in different positions and situations.

To improve mentality, the process is the same, with the exception that the skills you are improving are in your mind. They have an outward impact on the pitch, but those actions are a result of your internal mental processes – sometimes requiring an unorthodox approach to master, but possible to do none the less.

Implementing a good overall mentality in your game will be

virtually up to you. Being able to honestly assess your performance is difficult, but will help you improve. No one is perfect, and your ability to learn from your mistakes quickly, is a sign of a great player.

Implementation of improving mentality can come from a variety of methods: countless hours of film, individual training, team training, games and self-reflection. (Each of which works more powerfully in conjunction with one another.)

If video of your games is available, we highly recommend you watching. (Or begin to record so you can start watching.) The reason for watching film is for you to be able to see the game from a different perspective.

Doing so allows you to see your movement, your decision-making, your starting points, your effort etc. Soccer is a game that can be tough to quantify performance, so keep an open mind when watching film.

If you're unable to watch your own game film at the very least you need to be watching professional soccer games as often as possible. Watching others that play at a high level and then implementing what you take away from their game (both physical and mental) will help to expedite your soccer development.

Another helpful method on improving your mentality and work rate is through dialogue with your coaches. Coaches are a great resource to get feedback and learn from. They are the ones who watch your development of play most, and can give you reliable feedback as to how to improve your game.

When possible, ask your coach for an honest assessment of your game. Even if it is something you might not want to hear, it is necessary. Use his or her feedback as motivation to become a better player, and to improve on the things you need work on.

If there are some things you need to improve (and there always will be) ask the coach for different drills you can do on your own outside of training. Actively seeking help and wanting to improve will build character and further strengthen your mentality.

It is true when they say, " Mind over matter." Your mind controls everything, and recognizing what you need to do – **and then actually doing it**, is what separates the good players from the great ones.

SELF CONFIDENCE

Self confidence is the <u>mental state</u> a person has where they are certain or almost certain that a given event will occur. In the case of soccer, a player is sure that they have the ability to perform a certain action –beat a player, score a goal, make a save, win the game. Or that any number of soccer actions they elicit will result in their desired outcome.

Before we move further –yes we realize we just dedicated the entire previous chapter to improving your mentality, and confidence is technically a state of mind as mentioned above.

But, improving all the aspects of a positive mentality (Drive, Focus, Work Rate, Emotional Control, Visualization, Preparation) ties together with the end goal of building your soccer self confidence –and is why we consider it a key to soccer success that stands on it own.

Self confidence is so important in fact, that it can (and for many player does) over compensate for lacking aspects of your game.

Self confidence is a catalyst (I would dare say, a requirement) for playing at a high level; it is ultimately what separates average players from great.

Players across the best leagues in the world have similar technical abilities, there are outliers in both directions, but the largest thing that separates players within these leagues is their levels of self confidence.

A prefect example of what can happen to a player who looses their self confidence is former Athletico Madrid, Liverpool, and Chelsea striker Fernando Torres. In his prime, he was everything you wanted in a striker: pace, skill, and an eye for goal. During this time he was referred to as one of the best strikers in the world, who's confidence was at an all time high.

His 25 million pound transfer from Athletico Madrid to Liverpool only increased this confidence and he went on to score 65 goals in 102 appearances. This great form lead to another lucrative transfer fee of 50 million pounds to Chelsea. But it is here, where the high expectations of the new club turned his confidence sour.

With his new team Chelsea, we saw a completely different Torres. This low in confidence Torres was only good for 20 goals in 110 appearances. Nearly a third of the production with his former club!

There was nothing different this time around: he wasn't injured, he was still on one of the best teams in the world, was playing with some of the best players in the world, was still receiving quality passes and having plenty of opportunities to score goals.

But the one thing that changed, and we all saw it the longer he went without scoring goals –Confidence. It got so bad that you could literally see his lack of belief in his own abilities every time he received the ball. This is what a lack of confidence did to one of the best strikers in the world! It's that important.

Having high confidence allows you to play the game you want to play, and become the player you want to become.

As any player rises through the ranks in soccer, be that through youth, academy, college or pros there will regularly be times where you will be tested and have to trust in yourself to overcome any obstacles in your way –from self doubt, negative coaches, lack of motivation, criticism, taking chances and more. But what's most important is that you truly believe in your self and your abilities.

The biggest culprit for a lack of self confidence is due to one thing –**FEAR**.

There are many different factors that elicit this fear –which can be brought on by both external (coaches) and internal (self doubt) pressures, but in the end it comes down to fear of one thing:

A fear of making a mistake.

External factors create an environment that amplifies the underlining internal fear of making a mistake. Many times this is the case when coaches are overbearing or overly critical of your game.

Criticism from others, or times when you doubt your own abilities or goals in soccer are other aspects that will test your resolve and self believe.

You must never allow fear to disrupt your natural ability, or hinder your development. But above all else, **you must NEVER be afraid of making a mistake**. This is the true secret to soccer success.

You must be able to trust in yourself and not depend on a coach or any other outside factor for constant reinforcement, praise or motivation.

Failure to have trust and confidence in your own ability –or a self motivating drive, means there will quickly come a time when you are exposed to an obstacle that will be to great.

A lack of confidence (or fear of a mistake) in this situation is likely to lead to poor performance –if not complete failure.

At times through your soccer career it will almost feel like you need a degree in bravery to get through situations or to perform at a certain level within the game. However, all of the best players regularly take risks that pushed their limits both on and off the field.

This is not to say they do not have any fear while doing it, but they never allow that fear to prevent them from trying in the first place.

It may go against your initial instincts to try such things or have such self confidence, but this can only improve and build if you take

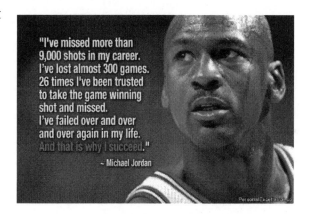

"I've missed more than 9,000 shots in my career. I've lost almost 300 games. 26 times I've been trusted to take the game winning shot and missed. I've failed over and over and over again in my life. And that is why I succeed."

– Michael Jordan

action in the first place. This is how building your confidence works –it's a self fulfilling loop:

Action > Mistake > Learn > Build > Grow > Confidence > Action >

(Fear is what prevents people from taking action in the first place.)

A perfect example of a top professional soccer player with complete soccer confidence would be Zlatan Ibrahimovic, the Sweden and current Paris St-Germain striker.

He has always expressed supreme confidence in his ability and as a result is always comfortable in any given situation on the pitch. He is happy to try innovative things and does not get troubled or stressed if something goes wrong – he has confidence that the next time will be better.

After Sweden's exit from the 2002 World Cup, despite having only recently broken in to the national side, Ibrahimovic loudly expressed that he would be the world's best striker before long. He always had a resounding confidence that he had all the tools to become great, that it was ultimately up to him to achieve success. Accepting failure was never an option.

He was right, he's been one of the greatest strikers in the world for the best part of a decade, and has won trophies with every team he has played for.

First Steps For Improving Your Soccer Confidence:

It is very easy to pick out everything you did wrong, and to make a bigger deal out of mistakes than needed. Yes, soccer players should be accountable and should hold themselves to a high soccer standard, but mistakes will happen and you need to be accepting and open to them. The best players in the world make mistakes; so don't think for a second you wont.

The first way to improve your confidence is to give positive feedback. Just like you tell yourself all the bad things you do, also tell yourself all the good.

According to the Harvard Review, research shows that the best ratio of negative feedback to positive is nearly 6 to 1.

This means for every one thing you feel needs improvement or you have negative criticism or thoughts about, you need six positives to find balance. (This is how powerful negative thoughts can be and why it can be the fastest way to torpedo your development.)

Approaching your training this way will go a long way because your perspective is focused on the improvements which will keep you moving forward. Rather than the negatives, self doubt and fear of mistakes that will hold you back.

You are a good player, and you have the capability of becoming great. Never doubt that! Have short-term memory about mistakes, learn from them and move on!

In addition to realizing that mistakes will be made, it is also vitally important how you react after making a mistake.

Plenty of players take a hit to their confidence and their first instinct is to "hide". By this we mean that they no longer make themselves available for a pass, no longer shoot in the same areas of the field, attempt to beat their opponent, remain a vocal presence on the field and so on.

This is one of the most destructive things a player can do not only to their confidence but also to their chances of success in soccer.

Ensure that you make a conscious effort to tell yourself that having made a mistake isn't a big deal and move on rapidly. Dwelling on mistakes will cause a spiraling effect of negative thoughts and actions, resulting in further mistakes and noticeably reduced levels of performance and confidence.

Worse still, by hiding in the game you are making it infinitely harder on yourself to stand out to coaches and/or scouts. If you do not constantly showcase or have belief in your talents then you will not have success – nobody will take somebodies word that you are a great player, they will expect to see it for themselves.

Positive reinforcement is good in that you allow yourself praise, or good treatment for what you have accomplished. Just like teams get trophies for winning, same can go for you and your personal achievements. But don't go overboard, still have a sense of reality for the work that needs to be put in to improve. Never get complacent.

How To Implement In To The Game:

Say for example, you seem to not be connecting on your passes and are giving the ball away a lot. What most players would do is hide and not want anything to do with the ball, because confidence is low at that point.

These players have insufficient confidence and will slowly let the game drift by, making no impact. Although the player may take relief in the bad feeling experienced from making the mistake, this will always result in having a negative impact on both the player and team.

Many players believe they can get away with it, but you cannot. Coaches and informed spectators are always able to spot a player hiding and the results are never good.

In the same situation highlighted above, a confident player would continue to want the ball, call for the ball, even demand the ball. Instead of hiding, the player is eager to prove that the last mistake was a one off, that they can make amends and ultimately show everybody their true quality.

Eventually, you will get out of the slump, and you will see that your game has improved. Never go quiet, always want the ball and continue to have self-belief. It may feel unnatural at first to continue to want the ball in these situations; however, the mind very quickly becomes accustomed to this way of thinking.

You can easily implement this just with a small mental note to yourself after every mistake. It is a simple technique but one that **will have a huge impact** on you as a player.

The goal is to reach a stage where you can enter every game or situation, regardless of importance, never being afraid to make a mistake. Have the belief and knowledge that every mistake is not a big deal or something to get worked up about.

Once you have the ability to shake off mistakes and experience the feeling of rectifying a mistake by proactively seeking out the ball or the next challenge, you will quickly develop incredible self-belief.

Even better, this self-belief can eventually lead to you

improving performance after making a mistake in the first place, almost using errors as a fuel to spur you on and drive better results.

Quincy is a great example of this, he has gotten to the point where he has trained himself to use mistakes as extra motivation rather than deflation. His most impressive play tends to come after making simple mistakes. You can use this same strategy to improve your play as well.

Improving team confidence:

You should now have a strong understanding that implementing confidence and belief in your own game is about positive reinforcement through **actions** and words. Doing the same for your team is no different.

You want to be relaxed and enjoying the game while playing. There is no better way to enjoy the game, than by also being a strong positive leader for your teammates while on the field.

Whether they make a good tackle, good pass, or score a goal; this will go a long way with your psyche, and the psyche of your teammates – it's almost contagious. That type of positive reinforcement will go a long way with helping you, as well as your team succeed.

Just as important to note is that positive reinforcement can also come after mistakes. We always want to be positive and support our teammates. Instead of yelling when someone makes a bad pass, build him or her up! Say something like, " Unlucky get the next one." Or, " nice try."

Any words of encouragement that prevent them from hiding (remember this is very bad to do!) and not wanting to receive the ball anymore are good.

Always think, would what you are about to say help you if you had been the one to make the mistake? It's a basic common sense question that we can sometimes forget to do. Soccer is a team sport and if one player fails, you all do.

Along the same lines, you cannot be a great player without the help of your teammates, make sure they are in the best possible mental shape to help you.

SOCCER IQ

Having a great understanding of the game is necessary to becoming a great soccer player. Knowing not only where **you** should be, but also where your teammates are – different formations, styles of play, and what best to do in any given situation is what we define as your "Soccer IQ."

Having a high soccer IQ makes the game easier and more enjoyable. It is also a great indicator to coaches of your maturation as a player. Being aware of what is around you and exactly how to overcome every obstacles the game presents is no easy task.

And as you progress through the various levels of soccer – every facet will become more complex and the time you have to make soccer decisions greatly decreases.

Coaches are quickly able to spot players that don't understand the intricacies of the game and having a low soccer IQ can result in "good players" never seeing the field.

Now your soccer IQ is a combination of a number of different things –but overall it is your understanding of these three main groups…

1. Individual Positioning and Movement (Both with/without the ball)

2. Team Positioning and Movement (Both with/without the ball)

3. Anticipation (or overall reading of the game)

In truth, a player needs to excel at all of the above in order to become great at soccer.

Although there are some players who make it far in the game without ever being exceptional at any of these, eventually they reach a ceiling and cannot improve beyond this. All of these aspects need to interlink with one another to some extent, though equally can be considered separately.

> ** Though we've narrowed down soccer IQ to 3 main categories, there is too much information to cover everything required to master soccer IQ in this book. Again, this book is meant to be an overhead view of the 9 keys to soccer success and we will be writing future books that will go in to full detail as how to master soccer IQ at a later time. The rest of this chapter will give you some great ways to start learning and implementing how to improve your soccer IQ.**

Individual positioning is perhaps the easiest or most commonly referenced attribute of soccer IQ. Regardless of formation, each player is given a position to play within a coach's system of play. In order to consistently play a successful part in the game, you must always be in the right place at the right time.

Having a solid basis of when and where you should be will help aid the other aspects of your soccer IQ. And will allow you more time to make the appropriate soccer decision for any given situation on the field.

This awareness of all traditional positions applies to the movements **both with and without the ball**.

With the ball; you must know when and where to pass, when it is appropriate to dribble, to shoot, to cross and so on.

Like we have mentioned, a lot goes in to developing your soccer IQ and knowing when and where to make the appropriate decision at any given time.

For example, if you are a defender and receive possession of the ball deep within your own half and under pressure from the opposing team, you should instinctively know that you should **not** dribble out of this position.

Dribbling here would result in a high risk of losing the ball in a dangerous area, with the opposition already closer to your goal than you are yourself.

This situation doesn't just apply to only being a high risk of dribbling either. Knowing if a pass, or if a certain type of pass should even be attempted is based on; your positioning relative to your teammates, what foot the ball is on, whether or not you are facing your own goal, your personal abilities to paly out of a specific situation, your risk tolerance, your coaches risk tolerance (or style of play) and more.

Now without the ball, movement is just as important but sometimes for different reasons. You must know when to make a movement forward (or backward) to create space for your teammates to pass (or dribble) and keep play going, and equally you must also know where to move if your teammate loses the ball.

Even though the ball may not be anywhere near you, your movement is crucial to the flow of the game. You could be forcing an opponent to track you to create space for others, you could be taking up a position to allow a chance to be created in another area of the field, or even to cover space to ensure that an opposing player cannot pass to a certain opponent or run into space you don't want them to.

Each individual's movement is key to the outcome of the game, no matter how trivial you think it may be at the time.

Here we can even link back to our earlier referenced skill – **work rate**. Plenty of players try to cheat themselves or teammates by not covering back on the defensive side of the ball, this lack of movement to cover off opponent's space can ultimately cost a team a goal.

Similarly, the same can be referenced for **self confidence** – if things are not going well with the ball, you can think about things you are doing well <u>off the ball</u>.

Use the fact that you have covered an attacker well to prevent a threat, or positioned yourself in such a place to prevent the opposition from starting an attack; leveraging implementing your soccer IQ as little positives to rebuild confidence for the next time you receive the ball.

These are just a few examples of not only the complexities of the game of soccer as a whole, but how developing a high soccer IQ can be intertwined with your ability to excel in any given situation on the soccer field.

Anticipation (or your overall ability to read the game and make decisions) is a key skill that allows you to implement good practices when moving throughout the field. It is the ability to predict and instinctively "know" what the current game situation is, and your ability to react accordingly.

It is crucial to being a step ahead of your opponent as it is quite literally just that; your ability to predict what is going to happen before it happens, enabling you to be ready to take advantage.

Anticipation can simply be intuitively knowing where the ball is going to be passed to or where a teammate or opponent is going to run, shoot or move. Being able to read the game well will give you a massive edge over your opponent.

It will make the game seem as though it is moving in slow motion, and compared other players it will seem as though you are in a number of places all at once. In truth, you are not, in fact people with excellent reading of the game often have to do less running.

All top soccer players have a great ability to read the game, although the ways in which they read it may differ.

For example, the way in which a defensive midfield player should read the game is much different than that of an attacking player. Players in the defensive position need to develop a great understanding of how to read where opponents will dribble or where they will attempt to make a pass.

Claude Makelele, former Real Madrid, Chelsea and Paris St-Germain defensive midfielder, was considered an expert at reading opponents and breaking down plays. Despite not having an abundance of pace, he could patrol the space in front of his defense and cut the ball out before it reached the opponents forwards. He did so purely by having an unbelievable reading of where the ball would be next and making his journey there before it was even played.

Other, more attacking players, have instinctive reading of the game in a different capacity. For example, top strikers are considered to have an innate ability to judge where the ball will end up and be first to react to it. Robert Lewandowski is a striker who does just that. He has the ability to not only react first to loose balls in the box, but also to any mistake that a defender may make. The untrained person would calk this up to luck, but it is actually a highly trained skill. One developed over a long period of time and countless repetition. This results in him being presented with more goal scoring opportunities than most other strikers.

How to improve:

Improving your Soccer IQ is possible, and crucial to your success. The most important underlying skill necessary to improving your soccer IQ can come in the form of doing soccer specific drills working on spatial awareness.

Center-midfield players usually have the highest soccer IQ's on the team, and can/should be able to read the game well. A large reason for this is that in order to play in center midfield, you must constantly be looking around and aware of everything going on around you at all times. You simply won't play in the midfield position for long if you are unable to develop a solid understanding of the game.

This is in contrast to defenders and goalkeepers where the vast majority of the game is played in front of them. And in the case of forwards, with their back to goal most of the time.

Regardless of your position on the filed, you need to develop a high level of spatial awareness. (Which in turn will greatly improve your soccer IQ.) The best way to do this is though working on drills that actively require you to take mental pictures of what is around you, and make proper decisions quickly, and repetitively.

A quick example of incorporating this would be requiring yourself to never receive the ball without first looking over your shoulder. This seems like a very simple thing, and it is, but most players develop a bad habit of never looking over their shoulder early in their soccer development and is unknowingly something that has huge implications the further you go in your soccer career.

Incorporate this in to **every single drill you do** until it is ingrained in your game, and becomes second nature. Similarly, when you don't have the ball, practice always being aware of what is going on around you. (Other players positioning/movement near and away from the ball, your positioning relative to your formation, passing lanes, angles etc.)

Another thing you can do to help improve you awareness is to get used to communicating (during the run of play) to other teammates that you believe are out of position, in danger, or can use more information. The more information, the better equip you and your teammates will be to make good decisions.

For example, you are playing in the center and the ball is on the right with the opposition. As well as facing the right to see the threat on this side, you should also quickly check over your left shoulder to see if the left side is exposed (Checking to see if there are runners posing a threat to get in behind your defense, should the ball be switched in the air.) If not, then you can do a few different things. Depending whether or not your teammate (right winger) has been beaten you may need to cover that space to now delay the attacker or make their play more predictable by forcing them down the sideline. OR you can communicate to your right back to step to the attacker while you fill in to a better position to help support if they are beaten by the attacker as well.

It is important to know when to deal with a problem yourself and when to communicate the problem to teammates who may be better positioned to deal with it themselves.

Like we have continually said, soccer is fluid and there is really never one correct answer or way to solve a problem on the field. The higher your soccer IQ, the better you'll be able to address each situation and figure out multiple solutions to your soccer problems.

** We'll also add a few videos in the bonus section to give some visuals of how to deal with varying situations on the field: www.perfectsoccerplayer.com/bonus

One other great way of improving your Soccer IQ/Awareness (and one that is highly underrated) is to watch a lot of soccer of other teams (preferably professionally), as well as **film of yourself**.

Watching other people (both in and outside your position) can help you see things you might not have been able to otherwise. Maybe another players movement in certain situations stands out for you. Or maybe it's their ability to tackle, their dribbling skills, when they decide to shoot, what cues they look for, tendencies, you name it.

Watching is just another way to become a student of the game, and will dramatically help you to improve. So watch as much as you can, as often as you can.

We know that depending on your circumstances watching your own games can be tough at times, but if at all possible, should be a must! Seeing yourself play is completely different than when you're actually in the game playing.

Watching from this different perspective will allow you to see what you did/do badly, and what you did/do great. Taking notes, and actively watching will help better prepare you for the next time you play, allowing you to be able to identify certain situations, and act accordingly.

Implementing in to the game:

Being able to implement better awareness in your game will come down to the repetition and effort you put in to improving your soccer IQ off of the field.

Remember, there isn't always a definitive answer in soccer, but (in certain situations) there are choices that are better than others. It is ultimately up to you to decide if what action you decided to take was a good decision or not.

Like we said, watching the game as much as possible will allow you to see what the best players do in certain situations so you can take that knowledge and add it to your own game.

You can take this to the next level by actually attending live games and watching a particular player that plays your position. Try to not just simply watch the flow of the game, but follow the player around and see what they do and where they are both on and off the ball.

For example, Quincy is a two way striker, so he tends to watch the movement and timing of forward player runs and their hold up play. Then works to implement their good moment into his game.

I'm a defensive midfielder so I like to watch how a particular player (depending on the teams formation) maintains his teams shape and what parts of the field they work to maintain possession in.

Now your ability to see these subtle nuances and apply them to your own game won't happen overnight, and will require countless hours of training a preparation. But like we have said and will continue to say, it is only through your commitment to what you do off of the soccer field (watching games, extra training, active preparation etc.) that will determine how far you'll be able to go in you soccer career

TECHNICAL ABILITY

Our number one goal of this book is to break the game of soccer down to the most important core fundamentals that will translate to improving your ability as a soccer player <u>as fast as possible</u>. Doing so will give you the largest number of opportunities to play the game at whatever level you would like to pursue. No matter what level you're shooting for your technical ability will be the one –Key Of Soccer Success that you can't afford not to master.

What we see tends to happen though, is that most aspiring soccer players watch players like Ronaldo and Ronaldinho, with all their tricks and fancy play and think that that's what it takes to become a top soccer player.

This is not the case at all!

Thinking this way will greatly deter you from developing the skills that will actually translate in to improving your game on the field.

Yes, tricks and skill moves are helpful and yes, these players and many like them have great technical ability; BUT it was first their mastery of the 3 Most Important Aspects Of The Game that allowed them to take their technical abilities to the next level. Without having these 3 core fundamentals in place **first**, these players would never be at the levels they are at.

What we've done in this chapter is taken what is actually required to be a successful soccer player on the field, and broken it down to the only 3 things you need to master in order to play at any level (youth all the way to the pros). We call this –

The 3 Pillars Of Soccer Success

If you ignore everything else in this book and only focus on these three thing (regardless of your position on the field) you will dramatically improve the only parts of your game that will actually make a difference in your soccer success.

Pillar 1.

First Touch (Ball Control) –

This is critical to your soccer development, everything you will do in the future of your soccer career will hinge upon the quality of your first touch –and will make or break every other aspect of your game.

Coaches pay close attention to your ability to control the ball and your poise in certain situations. They love to see players that can control the ball and play out of close quarters. Your first touch showcases your overall ability, and is your ability to create yourself as much time as possible under pressure. This goes for **EVERY POSITION** on the field.

Regardless of what position you play, you must be able to control the ball and set yourself up to make good decisions on the field. Without this ability you cannot become a good soccer player, it really is that simple.

Your ability to quickly and efficiently control the ball is one of the main components that will place you in the top class bracket of players or at the bottom.

Instant control of the ball makes the game much easier, it will allow you extra time to be a step ahead of your opponents in all you decision making. This one skill alone really will make the largest impact to your overall performance, so it should be practiced EVERY training session (structured or on your own) and EVERYDAY without fail.

There are a number of ways in which the ball can be controlled and in order for you to be confident in any game situation you must practice them all. In a game situation the ball will not always come to you in the perfect position to control with your favored foot. Good soccer players can control the ball with both sides of their feet (and both feet), knees, chest, head, basically any part of the body except for the arm and hand —but even some players are able to get away with using their hand to control the ball as well ;)

Players that do not manage to master the skill of ball

control are always at a disadvantage. Instead of controlling the ball the moment it arrives, time is wasted attempting to control the ball with several touches. By the time the ball is controlled they are immediately under pressure from the opposition, the good run of another teammate has been missed or a shooting opportunity has gone.

In contrast, by having good control you can essentially buy yourself more time to make the right decision on the pitch. Dimitar Berbatov, former Manchester United forward and Bulgaria International, was always considered a player that had mastery of the ball.

He was never blessed with a lot of pace but yet always seemed to be in space and have time on the ball. The reason for this was that he controlled the ball no matter where (or how) it came to him. Even in the penalty area he would often appear to have a lot of time to pick where to place his shot, making the opposition look like they had not closed him down or marked him well enough.

In truth, they didn't have a chance. The ball would be controlled and then moved on before there was any time for them to react.

Pillar 2.

Long and short range passing –

A skill that is taken for granted and needs to be another priority in your game. Dribbling may look good, but passing is the way in which the ball is circulated through the field. Coaches love players that can pass with precision at different distances. There are only a limited amount of situations where dribbling and shooting are the correct decision, whereas passing makes up the vast majority of the entire game.

If you cannot properly pass the ball, coaches and especially your teammates will not trust to give you the ball. You may have a great shot or great dribbling skills, but if people think there is a high chance that you will not pass or are incapable of completing a pass, your risk of turning over possession becomes too high.

If you are deemed to be a player that is a poor passer, you will receive the ball much less, preventing you from having an impact on both your individual and team performance.

Some players, professionals included, spend nearly all of the game only delivering short passes. (As the game may require this at times) But these player should still be able to deliver a long pass when required. The game of soccer is very fluid, circumstances and situations can change and develop at any moment. You therefore must have the ability to adapt at all times.

Pillar 3.

Finishing (Shooting/Goal Scoring)

Yes, most players would only attribute this to strikers and forwards, BUT if you are a player that has the ability to have poise and composure in the box, coaches view this as extremely beneficial. This applies to every position on the field and can be the difference between making the team, making the bench or playing in the game.

At the end of the day, after breaking down or analyzing everything that happens within a soccer game only one aspect really matters – goals. A team can have all the possession, defend perfectly, create lots of chances, but if they cannot score they **cannot win.**

As a result, players that can score goals are always highly regarded and will go far. We are not indicating that in order to be successful in soccer you must train as a forward player, but adding the ability to score when a chance arises will be a huge boost to your game at any position.

A perfect example of a player who has added this ability to their game is Frank Lampard. The center-midfielder's main duty in the game would be to keep possession and supply the more attacking players further up the field. He did this effectively through both long and short range passing.

However, he was largely considered to be just average at this rather than excellent. There were a number of players around that had better passing ability than the former Chelsea man.

So why was Lampard heralded as a Chelsea and England legend? Well, it is because he developed the ability to score goals. He learned to time his runs into the box perfectly and be unmarked to give himself easy chances, he learned to take good free-kicks and he learned how to effectively shoot from distance.

Lampard would finish each season with circa 20 goals or more. He became almost the first name on the team sheet at club and country, even despite there being more talented players out there. Goals win games and therefore any player that can contribute in this department will always be valuable.

What this means:

Being able to control the soccer ball, is like writing your name, it should become second nature. Having the core fundamentals of technical ability is high priority, and should be worked on at all times. The art of passing, first touch, and finishing is what makes up a good soccer player. The best in the world are exceptional at these qualities, and you should be striving to be the same.

There is no single player in the world that has mastered technical abilities to such an extent that they have stopped practicing. Even Cristiano Ronaldo and Lionel Messi still practice their core soccer skills every single day with the aim of constantly improving.

There should never be a time where you feel that you no longer need to practice or work on drills that will maintain or improve your technical ability. It is a constant and ongoing development from the moment you start to the moment you retire from the game.

** This brings me to a quick point I would like to emphasize before moving on to the next chapter –the importance of <u>not</u> playing out of your current technical abilities.

Playing outside of your technical ability is just another way of saying "Doing too much on the soccer field, or not playing your game."

Like we mentioned earlier in the book, a player like Iniesta isn't known for his tricks and ability to beat players with special moves. But what has made him considered one of the best midfielders in the world is playing within his abilities and doing the right things, in the right places, at the right times.

You can find just as much success doing the simple things as you can doing "fancy" things. If you begin to try to do too much or things you can't, it will become clear to coaches that you're not being honest with yourself, and your game.

Even worse, it can lead to a misrepresentation of your true talents –with coaches believing you are a poor/average player in a given position, simply because you have tried to influence parts of the game that should have been left to others.

This is a big problem I see players looking to impress coaches and teammates do. This does nothing but hurt your soccer development and chances of getting more play time. Focus on developing your specialty of the game. Coaches want players that will listen, know their limits, and play within themselves.

Yes, you should express yourself as much as possible and play your game, but remember, this book is meant to be a blueprint for creating the greatest number of opportunities possible to play soccer at every level –so know that coaches equally admire and value a very simple, clean game played.**

Drills to get you improving your technical ability:

We've compiled PDF print outs and a few videos of drills to help you get started improving these 3 key aspects of your game. To get access to these FREE resources please head over to:

http://www.PerfectSoccerPlayer.com/Bonus

QUICKNESS

All good soccer players have the ability to process a lot of external information quickly, allowing them the time necessary to make the correct decision before others have a chance to react.

There are two forms of quickness: **Mental Quickness**; the speed at which you take to make a decision, and **Physical Quickness**; the speed at which you can carry out an action.

Players that can quickly decide what is required of them in any given situation, or have the ability to physically act faster than their opponent, will always perform better in game situations.

In the previous chapter we mentioned Berbatov, a player that wasn't going to break any sprinting records, but did have a good career and was a top forward. His main "speed" came in the form of knowing instantly how and where to control the ball and where his teammates were for passes. The speed at which he could process his surroundings and make a decision allowed for more time for him physically.

In addition to mental quickness and speed, quickness in the traditional sense (physical) is also a huge asset in soccer. This does not necessarily mean that you have to be the fastest player around.

It does however, mean that having enough speed to beat a player, reach the ball first or even cause a defender to stay back due to the potential threat of speed –is a big plus for you to have or add to your game.

Equally, speed can be just as important for a defender for the same reasons. You may need to quickly turn and chase back, stop and run the opposite direction, quickly step to play an attacker offside or quickly cover space if your teammate has been beaten.

Unlike most sports where speed is normally measured in straight-lines, in soccer, you must have the explosive ability of acceleration and change of direction. The muscles and joints behave differently for these movements and as a result you must practice drills to maintain and improve this ability.

The key here is that these drills must be performed at full intensity in order to elicit any benefit. The only way to effectively train and improve your quickness is to perform the proper exercises at maximum effort; it is not like training a ball-based skill that can be done at varying pace.

This is why we emphasize the **need** for implementing the agility ladder to your training regularly.

How to improve:

We've compiled some resources to help you get started improving your soccer quickness. To get access to these FREE resources please head over to:

http://www.PerfectSoccerPlayer.com/Bonus

How to implement in to game:

As we have already mentioned, there are countless situations in which you'll need to utilize your mental or physical quickness. Earlier in the book we discussed Soccer IQ, this ties together as to **when** you should use your quickness.

Look at where you are on the pitch, can you attempt to touch the ball past an opponent and run into the space without immediate danger should it go wrong? If the answer were yes, then this would be a perfect example of when to demonstrate your quickness.

The key is instinctively knowing when and where to best use your speed. A soccer game is 90 minutes long, so you will not be able to perform the whole game at maximum intensity. It becomes important to have the reading of the game to understand **when** to perform at high intensity speeds.

Quickness in both decision making and pace should become an integral part of your training regimen. The training drills we've provided (www.perfectsoccerplayer.com/bonus) should provide you with the basics to perform these whenever required.

You must always refer to your game intelligence and reading of the game (Soccer IQ) in order to know when and how best to use these skills.

AGILITY

What good is speed if it has no control?

The game of soccer is such that your body is required to perform a number of movements and skills that are foreign to every day life. You are often needed to contort in a range of positions at different speeds, and these are only possible if your body and muscles are ready and prepared.

When speaking about agility we are referring to your overall body control at pace. In other words, your ability to maintain poise and balance at varying speeds.

Agility is only present if in unison with your quickness and speed, without the set each mean little individually. Agility itself can be broken down into one main aspect –**Balance.**

Balance is your ability to know and control where all your body parts are in relation to your movements at any given time. We mentioned that your body needs to contort into different positions to effectively play soccer; balance allows you to do this without falling or injuring yourself. <u>Agility</u> is how effective you are able to maintain this balance, at change of direction and speed.

For example, a long ball is hit in your direction and you determine that it isn't going to fall perfectly into your path and at your feet. Good balance will allow you to reach out to the ball, perhaps lifting one leg into the air to catch the ball on an extended foot, or lean backwards to control the ball on your chest.

Agility is the same scenario, but your ability to adjust and maintain your balance accordingly, **while in motion**.

As we've stated before, Andres Iniesta is not large in stature, not the most athletic, and not a speedy individual. But what he does have is an extremely high level of balance, skill, and knowledge of the game. His balance is that of a trapeze artist during a hurricane. The way in which he maneuvers out of tight situations is something to be studied and implemented to your game.

Because he is so fluid in his balance, it affords him opportunities to get on the ball and make good decisions. If you get a chance, go on YouTube and watch his highlights. But most importantly pay attention to his ability to be a well balanced soccer player without being the biggest or most athletic.

If a player does not have adequate balance they will not be able to best get their body into positions to control, pass, head or shoot the ball. Constant work both in the gym and on the training pitch should be done to both improve and maintain balance at all times. Just like training and building muscles, if balance is not worked on it can be lost.

The best and fastest way to improve your agility are drills that focus on your footwork and or balance while also incorporating touches of the ball.

This would be things like using your agility ladder while doing first touch, or change of direction drills. Or using a balance ball doing the same thing.

Drills to improve your agility:

We've compiled some PDF print outs of drills you can use to start improving your agility. To get access to these FREE resources please head over to:

www.PerfectSoccerPlayer.com/Bonus

Without incorporating the proper drills into your training regime you will not be able to maintain a high level of agility. Yes, you do have a natural base level, but even this declines over time if not practiced and worked on.

Just like shooting or passing would become worse if never practiced, so to does agility. It should be taken just as seriously and trained just as hard

FITNESS

Ok, so now you have a full understanding of what core attributes will turn you in to the complete soccer player, but now it's time we dive in to what will allow you to perform at this high level for as long as possible…

The first step in that process is getting your body to the best physical condition as possible –i.e. highest level of soccer fitness.

Having a high level of fitness isn't something that most soccer players don't think they need, or try not to implement. But we don't think players give as much thought to it as they should.

Being physically fit, and having a great engine will serve you well when playing soccer, and can almost be used as an "ace up your sleeve." Fitness is crucially important; as it is how coaches measure how reliable you will be throughout a 90 minute game. (and entire season)

Coaches need players who can run, be effective and be relied upon to help the team, NOT somebody who will struggle to play an entire game and require early substitution (Possibly limiting a coaches ability to make particular tactical decisions). If you are not able to consistently run, cover ground and last, a coach will be skeptical of playing you. Not only that, but a lack of fitness can make you more prone to injury as well.

Tired legs and tired minds are never poised for high performance. Your level of fitness needs to be a mainstay of your game, or will ultimately become something that will hinder your ability to excel at other parts of your game.

As a soccer player the game is most difficult (and your ability to make smart decisions is lowest) when you are fatigued. So implementing things that will allow you to avoid fatigue for as long as possible will greatly improve your overall performance.

How to improve:

The good news is that any player can greatly improve his or her fitness, regardless of current soccer ability. The only thing required is the desire, time and dedication to applying the proper fitness training program.

What is most important is that your fitness program tackles both aerobic and anaerobic systems. This is due to the fact that not only will you need to be able to run around for at least 90 minutes of normal play, but you must also be fit enough to perform a number of high intensity plays as required through the flow of the game. (and your position)

For example, a defensive midfielder may have been running at moderate pace (slow jog) for 5 minutes getting in to position to support his attacking teammates. Their team then loses possession and as a result that player has to make an immediate defensive sprint back in to position to prevent a counter attack.

Most of every game results in many scenarios just like the one highlighted above, this is why we greatly emphasis that you incorporate interval training in to everything that you do. This will be the basis for all your other soccer fitness development.

Interval training is just a fancy way of saying, incorporating drills, runs and movements that vary in speed, intensity and duration throughout your training.

8 week fitness program:

We've added an 8 week preseason fitness program to the bonus section of our members area. This is the very program we are given for our professional offseason. To get access to these FREE resources please head over to:

www.PerfectSoccerPlayer.com/Bonus

Your fitness is completely dependent on how much time and dedication you are willing to spend on the training pitch. We know how easy it can be to cheat this part of your game; **<u>but don't do it!</u>**

Quincy hates working on his fitness and is the one thing he dreads doing the most. I on the other hand enjoy running, so working on fitness comes fairly natural to me. Though we both personally feel different about fitness, our stance on the importance of your level of fitness is the same.

Come game day it will be clear to coaches where your fitness stands. Be proactive about your fitness training and you'll have nothing to worry about in the game.

RECOVERY

In soccer, the physical, mental, and emotional demands of the game will always be there; and if gone unchecked can (and will) become overwhelming. Being a great soccer player is a 24/7 365 day a year gig, with NO EXCEPTIONS. Sure, you might not be a professional player (yet!), but you should always act and conduct yourself as one.

The single largest thing you can do as a player to not only consistently paly at a high level, but also prolong the length of your career is though implementing proper recovery into your training regimen.

This preparation encompasses the food you eat, the sleep you get, and the rehab you endure. The care you take for your body and mind is what will allow you to perform at your best for as long as possible.

"What you put in is what you get out."

There are many different methods that promote recovery. Here is a list of things you can do to aid your body and mind in that process:

-Sleep

-Nutrition/Supplementation/Hydration

-Rehab

    -Ice Baths

    -Massage

    -Yoga

    -Training Room/Treatment

    -Compression Wear

    -Meditation

    -Foam Roll

    -Stretching

    -Light Swimming

    -Cycling

Sleep is the time the body needs to regenerate due to the stress put on the body while playing and training. Generally speaking, 7-8 hours of sleep will do the body good, and will be beneficial during a long season. Most of the repairing of muscles is done during this time, so by not getting enough sleep you are immediately hindering your body's ability to regenerate and be fully ready for the next training session or game.

Nutrition, speak to your coach and a nutritionist in more detail as to the specifics of your diet. There are guides and meal plans of what to eat, but as each individual has different needs and different metabolisms it is best to have this customized to your personal needs.

That being said, a solid rule of thumb is to approach with the "everything in moderation" method. During your training you will be burning calories and breaking down muscle fibers, you need to be eating to replenish this, and to build and repair.

Professional players are very particular about what foods they eat not only in the build up to a game, but day to day in general.

Hydration –It should also not be understated how important fluids are to this recovery. You must be replenishing the water (and electrolytes) your body loses throughout training and games. Dehydration is a common cause of under performance and only a fraction of players ever realize this fact. Be smart and always maintain your water levels.

Supplementation is exactly that, supplementing. It is not meant to be a replacement for a standard diet, nor should you just take anything on the market. There are rules and regulations you need to follow depending on the level you play, but more importantly you never want to be taking anything that could have adverse affects to your health. Be sure to check out the bonus section (www.perfectsoccerplayer.com/bonus) where we'll add some additional (regularly updated) materials on the best supplements specific for soccer players.

Rehab –getting the right treatment and taking care of your body and mind off the field is huge. (The extra time you dedicate to this will impact how long you'll get to play the game of soccer for.)

Doing so will allow you to recover as quickly as possible, stay fit, and stay strong. Foam rolling, massages, ice baths, stretching and yoga are great ways to help your muscles recover and get the attention they need. They may not all be pleasant experiences; in fact most are the opposite of pleasant. But, the fact remains that they are important, they will help you, and you will reap the benefits.

Compression wear is a new way in which players are trying to gain another advantage in recovery. This involves wearing tight (specially designed) fitting clothes or wraps which support and compress muscles and joints. In addition to recovery these can sometimes be used as a prevention or aid to allow a player to train or play despite some discomfort in the muscle. **ALWAYS speak to your coach and physiotherapist about an injury before attempting to play through a potential injury with aids such as these.

Meditation –something that is slowly beginning to gain attention throughout high level soccer circles. As we dedicated the entire first chapter of this book to Mentality, it should be no surprise that we highly recommend implementing meditation to your game. There are many resources out there that can help you begin the process of learning how to meditate and the many benefits it brings. One place you can start is by downloading an app called HeadSpace on your mobile device. (As of the writing of this book there is a free 14 day trial)

…

Outline which methods you would like do to aid in your recovery and begin implementing them right away. Maybe you don't like cold baths, so you just get ice instead. Maybe there are certain foods you do not enjoy, so you work with a nutritionist to find other foods to supplement for them. Staying organized will help, and will be a great reminder for you to stay on track. Remember, this is a 24/7 365 gig, NO EXCEPTIONS.

Find a system that works for you and stick to it. Avoid the temptations to skip or ignore things that you dislike and do not want to do. Always remind yourself that the aim of everything you do is to help you improve as a player, get you where you want to be, and to achieve your soccer goals. The methods and techniques are clear to follow if you stay organized. The main challenge is to conquer the mental side and keep on track.

The time you dedicate to your recovery will be seen (and felt) during the games, as well as after. Committing to take care of your body and mind will pay dividends. You will still be tired and fatigued after practice and games, but not as much as you would be otherwise.

You will also recover between games and sessions a lot quicker, and be ready to take on any soccer obstacles in your path. Once you start feeling the benefits of implementing great recovery habits you'll never not continue doing so in the future.

TIME MANAGEMENT

If you begin to implement everything required to become a better soccer player, you'll quickly realize that it is a **big time commitment.** Which ends up meaning you need one additional skill to truly succeed. It is what will bring everything we've spoken about throughout this entire book together –Soccer Time Management.

Having a set regimen will best prepare you for soccer success. This point is so important yet undervalued we wanted to make it a complete chapter of its own **–It's that important!** The reason this is at the end of the book is not because of it's lack of importance, BUT the need for you to first understand each block it takes to build a great soccer player, BEFORE then learning how to best bring it all together.

Managing your time is a vital life skill and one of the most important skills to achieve soccer success (or success in anything else for that matter).

Players who have soccer on top of a busy school and/or work schedule know how stressful things can get. Time is the most important assets you own, so it's extremely important to manage it as effectively as possible.

Never be the player that says they, "don't have enough time".

Unless you're married, have kids, a full-time job, a second part time job and have to look after someone with a serious medical problem –then you're most likely making excuses for why you aren't at the level you say you want to be in soccer.

There are 168 hours in a week. Let me highlight that again.

168 hours!

Let's break down all the time most people say they don't have for a second, and see what's left over. I'll even be very generous with the numbers here:

Let's say you have school and homework or a full-time job which takes up an average of 40 hours a week. You sleep an average of 8 hours per night, and you sleep in a few extra hours more on the weekends (10 hours on Saturday and Sunday).

You spend 10 hours a week on the essential stuff like showering, eating, commuting and using the bathroom.

On top of that, you spend 20 hours a week playing video games, texting, Facebooking, Instagramming, watching movies, hanging out with friends, etc. Oh, and just for fun let's add on that you also work a part-time job at your local café which takes up an additional 10 hours a week.

And finally an additional 5 hours for just staring off in to blank spaces (because you decide to get really in to that for some reason).

Even after all of this you still have **23 hours per week** left to do whatever you want! This is time you can dedicate solely to your craft, on getting really good at something. And if you don't have a part-time job and take video games, social networks and staring in to space out of your life, well you actually have **58 hours per week** of free time.

So you have to ask yourself, do you really not have enough time to make this work? How much time am I going to dedicate to getting better at soccer? 5 hours a week? 10? 15? 20? How can you make time everyday to train?

Soccer training schedule time management template:

We've added a sample soccer training time management template for you to use to help you get the most our of your individual training schedule. To get access to these FREE resources please head over to:

<u>www.PerfectSoccerPlayer.com/Bonus</u>

Be Disciplined!

Soccer academies and high level teams are not very friendly in terms of being flexible with time, so if you're serious about improving you game (and we know your are) you'll need to get creative with your individual training schedule. If you're not on a team or part of an academy, you have the freedom to decide when and where you want to train. It's cool to have that freedom, however what you do in both cases will require a high level of discipline.

It's nice to create yourself a training schedule, BUT the only way for it to be effective is if you commit to it under all circumstances! No matter if you feel tired, lazy, it's raining or cold outside, you have to make the personal choice that you **will do it** and **stick to it**.

What I did to make sure I trained a minimum of 20 hours a week by myself (on top of my team trainings) was by making a promise to myself. I would give hold myself accountable by literally writing down:

"If I don't do 20 hours of training by 11:59pm Sunday, I will ban myself from playing FIFA and watching TV for one week"

"For every hour of training I miss this week, I must do triple the following week."

So if I missed two hours of training this week, I'd add on an additional six the next week. There were a couple of times I grudged out 40 hours of additional training, but this did nothing but further help me improve my game so it was a win-win. Making promises to yourself like this is not the easiest task, but having a discipline system in your life will change how much you achieve.

Additional tips for staying disciplined:

Do your training first thing in the morning –this can be tough to follow if you're not a morning person. Personally, I like to sleep in and go to sleep late if I have the choice. But before you eat breakfast or your day starts, do you training. You will feel good for the rest of the day knowing that you improved yourself and you can go through the rest of your day without stressing over the training you still have to do by the time you get back home after a long day.

(Quincy wrote a good article about implementing a morning routine that can help you get started. You can go here to read it: http://quincyamarikwa.com/morning-routine/)

Keep a diary –keeping track of where you've been and how far you've come is crucial for improving the quickest and most effective way. After training sessions and matches, jot down notes on a piece of paper or in your phone on what you did good/bad and how you feel.

After a few weeks, you'll start seeing a pattern of your (then-current) strengths, weaknesses and certain feelings. Because your short-term goals are always changing, you'll start seeing certain aspects of your game being a problem and then slowly fading away until they actually become strengths.

During my time in high school I sat down and wrote in my journal every single week. I owe doing this to improving so quickly. This is still something I do in my own time to this day.

The Weekly Review:

If you choose to implement having a soccer diary you can begin to structure your diary writing so it has two parts:

1. This week –

-**Training:** How did training go? Was it effective? Did you feel improvement?

-**Game Performance:** How did your performance in game go? Did you score/assist/play consistent? What was good/bad?

-**Short Term Goals Review:** Take notes of your short-term goals.

-**Life:** What's up with your personal life? How's school/work going? How do you feel about yourself? What are you excited about right now? What are you worried about?

-**Other:** Did you watch any games this week? What caught you eye? Any final thoughts?

2. Next Week –

-What you will do in training next week? What do you
want to get out of it?

By the time Sunday evening comes around, sit down and
look at all the notes you've taken during the week and
reflect on how everything went. Then write down in full
how you feel and try to be as honest with yourself as
possible. This way you'll be about to look back weeks or
moths later and know exactly how you were feeling at the
time and be able to create a solid plan of attack for the
future.

With a journal you can clarify your thoughts and feelings,
know yourself better, reduce stress and solve problems
more effectively.

FINAL THOUGHTS

If you are to take one thing away from this guide, let it be that not one of these nine key attributes will come to fruition by themselves. Each requires dedication and persistence. These two factors will be key not only to improving and becoming great, but also maintaining and improving your ability once you have reached a particular goal you have set for yourself.

Both Quincy and I reached our goal of becoming professional soccer players; did this mean that we stopped working on any of these key fundamentals? No, in fact, the opposite is true. The time we dedicate to our craft has only grown over the years and if your goal is to get to the same level, you must always be prepared to continue to work and develop as a player.

You will see that a lot, if not all, of these nine keys interlink with one another –feeding off each other in a way that results in your overall level of soccer ability. This highlights how important it is to ensure that you work on ALL aspects of your game.

We have highlighted throughout the book that simply having a good shot, pass, positional sense, or whatever, is not enough on its own. You must always strive to be as good as you possibly can in every aspect of your game.

Work hard, be dedicated, put in the hours on the training pitch and follow the guidelines set out in this book. If you do, you will greatly improve and get to whatever level you wish to achieve!

****

FOR GRABBING A COPY OF OUR BOOK WE'D ALSO LIKE TO EXTEND YOU A 10% DISCOUNT **CODE: PS9KEYS** TO ANY AND ALL SOCCER TRAINING EQUIPMENT PURCHASED OVER AT:

http://www.PerfectSoccerSkills.com

And be sure to get all your FREE bonuses and downloadable materials for purchasing our book by heading over to:

http://www.PerfectSoccerPlayer.com/Bonus

Thanks!

Ross LaBauex and Quincy Amarikwa

Made in the USA
Middletown, DE
13 February 2017